Comparing
People From
the Past

Christopher
Columbus and
Neil Armstrong

Nick Hunter

Raintree is an imprint of Capstone Global Library Limited, a company incorporated in England and Wales having its registered office at 7 Pilgrim Street, London, EC4V 6LB – Registered company number: 6695582

www.raintreepublishers.co.uk
myorders@raintreepublishers.co.uk

Edited by Clare Lewis, Linda Staniford and Abby Colich
Designed by Philippa Jenkins
Original illustrations © Capstone Global Library Ltd 2015
Illustrated by HL Studios, Witney, Oxon
Picture research by Gina Kammer
Production by Victoria Fitzgerald
Originated by Capstone Global Library Ltd
Printed and bound in China

ISBN 978 1 406 28988 6 (hardback)
18 17 16 15
10 9 8 7 6 5 4 3 2 1

ISBN 978 1 406 28993 0 (paperback)
19 18 17 16 15
10 9 8 7 6 5 4 3 2 1

British Library Cataloguing in Publication Data
A full catalogue record for this book is available from the British Library.

Acknowledgements
We would like to thank the following for permission to reproduce photographs: Bridgeman Images: Index/Private Collection/The 'Pinta', the 'Nina' and the 'Santa Maria' sailing towards the West Indies in 1492, from The Discovery of America, 1878 (colour litho), Spanish School, (19th century), 14, Private Collection/The First Voyage (colour litho), Searles, Victor A. (fl.1892), 12; Corbis: Bettmann, 10; Glow Images: Eric SA House - Carle, 4, cover (left); HL Studios: 15, 16; iStockphotos: ConstanceMcGuire, 9, Grafissimo, 28; Library of Congress: 19; NASA: 6, 7, 13, 20, 21, 24, 29, cover (right), JPL-Caltech/Malin Space Science Systems, 25; Newscom: akg-images, 22, CD1 WENN Photos, 27, Prisma/Kurwenal/Album, 23, Sipa USA/NASA/SIPA USA, 11, World History Archive, 17;North Wind Picture Archives: 8, 18; Nova Development Corporation (compass design): throughout; Shutterstock: e X p o s e, 5, Quaoar, 1, cover (background), spirit of america, 26.

Every effort has been made to contact copyright holders of material reproduced in this book. Any omissions will be rectified in subsequent printings if notice is given to the publisher.

All the internet addresses (URLs) given in this book were valid at the time of going to press. However, due to the dynamic nature of the internet, some addresses may have changed, or sites may have changed or ceased to exist since publication. While the author and publisher regret any inconvenience this may cause readers, no responsibility for any such changes can be accepted by either the author or the publisher.

Contents

Some words are shown in bold, **like this.** You can find out what they mean by looking in the glossary.

Who was Christopher Columbus?

Christopher Columbus was one of the most daring explorers. In 1492, he led an **expedition** across the Atlantic Ocean. Before he travelled there, nobody in Europe knew the continents of the Americas existed.

We cannot be sure what Columbus looked like as portraits like this were painted after he died.

European explorers found great cities and buildings in the Americas, such as this pyramid built by the Incas.

After Columbus's voyage, Europeans explored and settled in many parts of North and South America.
They often fought with the people who were already living in the Americas.

Who was Neil Armstrong?

Neil Armstrong was also an explorer. He was the first person to walk on the Moon. He knew where he was going, but he did not know what he would find there. His was a voyage into the unknown.

This photo of Armstrong was taken just before his voyage to the Moon.

Astronauts blasting into space on rockets like this could not be certain what they would find.

In 1961, the first **astronaut** blasted into space. Astronauts wanted to discover the secrets of space. Landing on the Moon was the greatest success of the space age.

Early life

Columbus was born in 1451 in the port of Genoa, Italy. The city was home to **merchants** and sailors, telling stories of their voyages. Columbus's family were wool merchants.

Trading ships brought **exotic** goods to Genoa from distant lands.

Christopher and his younger brother, Bartholomew, moved from Italy to live in Portugal.

When he was a teenager, Columbus went to sea. He sailed the coasts of Europe and Africa, learning about **navigation** and the ocean. He travelled as far as Iceland, living through storms and shipwrecks.

Armstrong was born in 1930 in Ohio, USA. He was always fascinated by aeroplanes. Armstrong did odd jobs to pay for flying lessons. He gained his pilot's licence on his sixteenth birthday.

When he was just two, Neil's father took him to see the air races in Cleveland, Ohio.

Armstrong joined the US Navy as a pilot. In 1950, Armstrong's plane was shot down while he was fighting in the Korean War. After the war, Armstrong tested new and **experimental** planes.

Young explorers

Columbus believed he could find a new route to the rich lands of Asia, but he needed money for his **expedition**. The King and Queen of Spain agreed to help him.

Columbus promised King Ferdinand and Queen Isabella of Spain that he would find them new lands to rule.

Armstrong had to make an emergency landing after some equipment failed on his *Gemini* spacecraft.

Armstrong joined the US space programme in 1962. He made his first space flight in 1966. The US president wanted an American to land on the Moon. It would take many years to plan the voyage.

Voyages of discovery

Columbus set off with three ships on 3 August 1492. He thought the voyage would take a few days. A month passed and they had still not seen land. Columbus's men became scared and upset.

Columbus's three ships were called the *Niña*, the *Pinta* and the *Santa Maria*.

This map shows Columbus's voyage. Columbus's own map did not show the Americas.

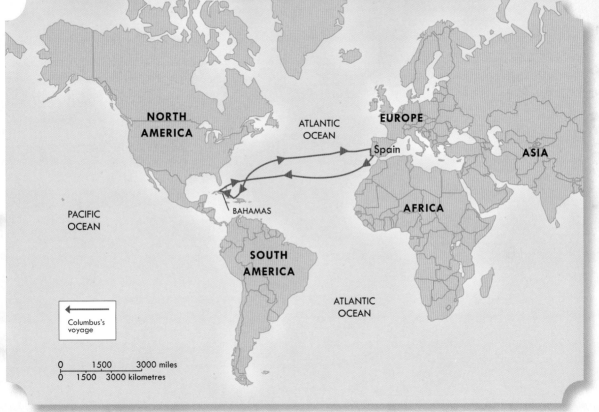

NORTH AMERICA

ATLANTIC OCEAN

EUROPE

Spain

ASIA

PACIFIC OCEAN

BAHAMAS

AFRICA

SOUTH AMERICA

ATLANTIC OCEAN

Columbus's voyage

0   1500   3000 miles
0   1500   3000 kilometres

After 36 days at sea, food was starting to run out. Then a lookout saw an island. Columbus went ashore. The island was part of the Bahamas.

Apollo 11 lifted off on 16 July 1969 carrying Armstrong, Edwin "Buzz" Aldrin and Michael Collins. People across the world watched this exciting moment on TV. The voyage to the Moon took four days.

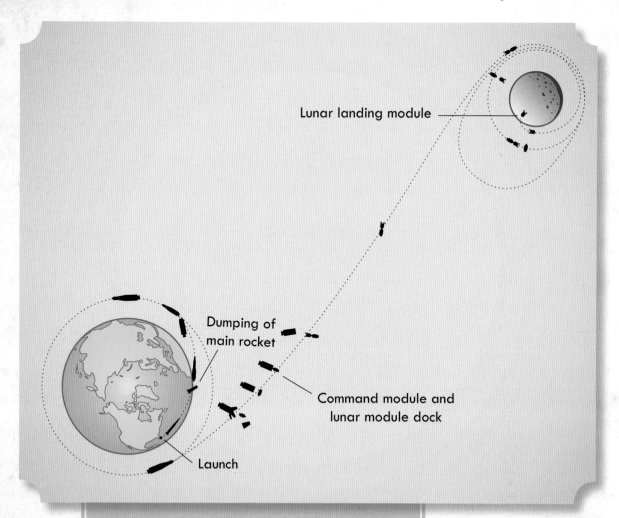

Lunar landing module

Dumping of main rocket

Command module and lunar module dock

Launch

Only a small part of the rocket that blasted off actually landed on the Moon.

This photo of Armstrong on the Moon was taken by Edwin "Buzz" Aldrin.

Armstrong had to pilot the lunar landing module on to the Moon's rocky surface. As he stepped from the spacecraft, he said, "That's one small step for a man, one giant leap for **mankind**."

What were their voyages like?

Columbus's ships were crammed with about 90 men, and constantly let in water. The *Santa Maria* was shipwrecked while Columbus explored the island of Hispaniola. Some of the crew had to stay on the island.

After the wreck of the *Santa Maria*, Columbus returned to Spain with just two ships.

Columbus called the local people he met Indians, because he thought he had discovered new lands in the East Indies.

The people who lived on the islands were friendly at first. When Columbus claimed their lands for Spain, these people tried to fight off the Spanish invaders.

Life on *Apollo 11* was very cramped. People and objects float in space because the force of **gravity** there is weaker than on Earth. Special packaging and equipment helped the crew to stop their food floating around.

Pictures **transmitted** back to Earth showed that even simple tasks, like making a sandwich, were difficult to do in space, because of weaker gravity.

After returning to Earth, Armstrong and the other **astronauts** had to stay in **quarantine** for 21 days. This made sure that they had not brought unknown germs back from the Moon.

Changing times

After Columbus's voyage, other explorers set sail for the New World he had discovered. They brought back to Europe gold, silver, and new foods, such as potatoes. Some Europeans stayed in the Americas.

America was named after Amerigo Vespucci, who explored the continent in 1499.

Spanish explorer Hernán Cortés is seen here attacking the Aztec people of Mexico in 1520.

Columbus and those who followed him were interested in finding new lands and riches. They claimed the New World as their own land. They attacked the local people or forced them to work as **slaves.**

Armstrong was the first of only 12 people to visit the Moon. The last Moon landing was in 1972. Since then, **astronauts** have learned more about space. They hope to be able to land on Mars one day.

Astronauts can leave their spacecraft to do experiments and make repairs.

The *Curiosity* rover landed on Mars in 2012.

New technology helps scientists to explore space without travelling there themselves. Robots can explore parts of space that are too far away or too dangerous for astronauts to visit.

Growing old

Columbus sailed to the Americas four times. He still hoped to find China. The gold he brought back made him a rich man but because of his actions, many American Indians were badly treated. He died in Spain in 1506.

This statue in Italy shows Columbus pointing towards America.

After his amazing journey, Armstrong became one of the world's most famous people.

Armstrong did not seek fame. He knew that his incredible journey was a team effort by the **astronauts** and hundreds of scientists. He became a teacher at university. Armstrong died in 2012.

Comparing Christopher Columbus

Christopher Columbus

Born	1451
Died	20 May 1506

Exploration

Four voyages from Spain to Caribbean, Central and South America

Fascinating fact

Columbus never actually visited the mainland of North America.

Famous people living at the same time

- Leonardo da Vinci (artist and scientist, 1452–1519)
- Henry VII (first Tudor King of England, 1457–1509)
- Vasco da Gama (explorer, discovered route from Europe to India, 1460–1524)

CHRISTOPHER COLUMBUS

1400   1500   1600   1700

and Neil Armstrong

Neil Armstrong

Born	5 August 1930
Died	25 August 2012

Exploration

Two spaceflights including the *Apollo 11* mission to the Moon (July 1969)

Fascinating fact

Many things have been named after Armstrong, including an asteroid and a crater on the Moon.

Famous people living at the same time

- Nelson Mandela (political campaigner and South African president, 1918–2013)
- Queen Elizabeth II (queen of the United Kingdom, 1926–)
- Elvis Presley (musician, 1935–1977)

NEIL ARMSTRONG

1800   1900   2000

Glossary

astronaut someone who travels into space

exotic from another part of the world

expedition journey or voyage made for a reason

experimental not yet fully tested

gravity force that attracts smaller things to larger ones, such as planets

mankind word meaning all people on Earth

merchant someone who buys and sells goods

navigation finding your way using maps or other equipment

quarantine period of time that someone is kept away from others in case they pass on a disease

slave someone who is forced to work for no pay and is not free to leave

transmit send information electronically

Find out more

Books

Christopher Columbus (History Heroes), Damian Harvey (Franklin Watts, 2014)

How To Be a World Explorer, Joel Levy (Lonely Planet, 2012)

Neil Armstrong (Science Biographies), Catherine Chambers (Raintree, 2014)

New Worlds and Space (Explorer Tales), Nick Hunter (Raintree, 2012)

Websites

www.bbc.co.uk/schools/primaryhistory/
famouspeople/christopher_columbus/
Discover more about Columbus's life and voyages in this BBC biography. The website also includes a Columbus game.

www.cbsnews.com/news/neil-armstrong-first-man-on-the-moon-dead-at-82/
CBS TV news looks at the story of Armstrong's life.

www.nasa.gov/multimedia/hd/apollo11_hdpage.
html#.Uuj0Vnk4l1M
Watch videos of Armstrong's first step on the Moon.

Index